MW01681177

Only Speak What You Want To See

MRS. JAE AFAT

Scripture quotations are from the Holy Bible.

Dedication

I want to first thank God for being my everything. I owe everything to Him. I thank God for those He has ordained to read this and put it into action. I declare that their lives will change for the better and never be the same.

I thank my husband Troy for being so supportive and covering me in prayer.

I thank those 1%er's that encouraged me to write this as soon as the words "Only Speak What You Want To See" came out of my mouth.

Introduction

You ever talked to someone and their whole conversation was about everything going wrong? The bad doctor's report. The ache in their knees. The noise the neighbors make. On and on it goes. And the longer they talk, the heavier you feel — like the air itself is getting thick.

Then they turn to you and say, "If it ain't one thing it's another, right?"

And you nod. You agree. Because after sitting through that entire list, what else could you say? It sounds about right. It feels like the truth. And besides — it's just common courtesy.

But do you know what just happened? You came into agreement with something that you do not want to see in your life. And in doing so, you gave it access to your life.

This is not a small thing. The Word of God says you will be held accountable for every word that comes out of your mouth. Every. Word. That means words are not throwaway things. They are not just sounds that disappear into the air. They carry weight. They carry power. And they carry consequence.

I know that feeling because I lived it. My own prayer life once sounded exactly like that conversation. I would come before God exhausted and overwhelmed, laying out every problem, every fear, every burden — telling Him everything that was wrong. And that part is not incorrect. Jesus Himself said "Come to me, all you who are weary and burdened, and I will give you rest. My yoke is easy and my burden is light." So bringing it to God was never the mistake.

But I was stopping too soon. I was begging for something I had already been given. I thought laying it down and waiting for Him to fix it was the full basis of prayer. What I did not yet understand was that God had already answered my prayer — years ago, on the cross. What I needed to do was stop recounting my problems and start declaring His promises.

Instead of saying "God, people are talking about me and I don't know what to do, please help me, I feel so helpless" — I learned to pray like this:

> *"Lord God, You said that no weapon formed against me shall prosper, and every tongue that rises against me in judgment I shall condemn. I believe Your Word, Father, and I declare that every word spoken about me speaks of my integrity. Because I AM honest. Every word spoken about me speaks of how I care for people. Because I AM love. My name is synonymous with truth, honesty and love. Because I AM."*

That shift changed everything. And that is exactly what this book is about — learning to **only speak what you want to see.**

Chapter 1 — Watch Your Mouth: The Words We Inherited

From the time we were born, words were being poured into us.

From our parents. From our friends. From teachers, mentors, coaches and authority figures of every kind. Each one of them came from their own background, their own experiences, their own successes, as well as their own pain and their own limitations. And woven into everything they taught us were words — traditional sayings, common expressions, phrases passed down from generation to generation like family heirlooms. Except some of these were not gifts. They were chains.

> *"If it ain't one thing it's another."*
> *"When it rains it pours."*
> *"Nothing good ever lasts."*
> *"That's just how life is."*

You have heard these. You have probably said these. And if you are honest, some of them feel true — because in your life, they have played out over and over again. But have you ever stopped to ask yourself why?

Here is the answer. These words were spoken over you, about you and around you so many times that they became second nature. You were not born believing that life was one problem after another. You learned it. You heard it so many times, from so many people you trusted, that it stopped sounding like an opinion and started sounding like a fact. Like just the way things are. Like a part of who you are.

But it was never a fact. It was a seed.

The Word of God tells us in Romans 10:17 that "faith comes by hearing." Most people apply that scripture only to church — only to hearing the Gospel. But the principle is bigger than that. Whatever you hear repeatedly, you will eventually believe. And whatever you believe, you will speak. And whatever you speak — you will see.

This means the opposite is also true. Fear comes by hearing. Lack comes by hearing. Limitation comes by hearing. If you heard all your life that nothing ever goes right, you believed it. And because you believed it, you spoke it. And because you spoke it, you created a life that confirmed it — not because it was God's plan for you, but because your words built it brick by brick without you even realizing it.

This is not about blaming the people who poured those words into you. Your parents, your teachers, your mentors — they spoke what they knew. They passed down what was passed down to them. The cycle is older than any of us. But today, with the Word of God in your hands, the cycle stops.

Because now you know. And knowing changes everything.

The Moment I Noticed

Awareness is everything. You cannot fix what you cannot see.

For me, the shift began when I started paying attention. Not just to what others were saying — but to what I was agreeing with. I began to notice that in the middle of an ordinary conversation, someone would lay out everything going wrong in their life, and then turn to me expecting me to co-sign it. To nod. To say, "You're right, it's always something."

And I had done it a thousand times without thinking.

But once you see it, you cannot unsee it. I started to realize that agreement is powerful. When two or more people come into agreement, something is established. The Word of God confirms this — "if two of you agree on earth about anything they ask, it will be done." That principle does not only work in prayer. Agreement in conversation carries weight too. When you agree with negativity, you are not just being polite. You are giving it a foothold in your life.

So I stopped.

Not rudely. Not with a lecture. I simply stopped agreeing with what I did not want to see in my life. And I started countering with my truth. When someone would say "if it ain't one thing it's another" and look to me for agreement, I would simply say — "not for me. All things work together for my good."

Romans 8:28. That became my counter. My shield. My declaration.

It sounds simple. But try it and you will find out quickly that it is one of the hardest things you will ever do — because everything around you, every tradition, every old saying, every well-meaning person in your life will push back. The pressure to agree is real. But so is the power of your words.

You were not built to co-sign darkness. You were built to declare light.

How To Counter

So how do you actually do this? How do you break a habit that has been forming since childhood? How do you stop agreeing with what you have always agreed with and start declaring what you want to see instead?

It starts with three things. Awareness. Decision. Declaration.

Step 1 — Awareness

You cannot change what you do not notice. So the first step is simply to start paying attention to your words. Not just in prayer — but in everyday conversation. At the dinner table. At work. In the car. On the phone. Listen to what you are agreeing with. Listen to what is coming out of your mouth. Are your words describing the life you have or declaring the life you want? Start there. Just listen. You may be surprised — even shocked — at what you have been speaking without realizing it.

Step 2 — Decision

Once you see it, you have to make a decision. A firm, settled, non-negotiable decision that you will no longer come into agreement with what you do not want to see in your life. This is not about being negative toward people or shutting down every conversation. It is about guarding what you allow to take root in your spirit through your own mouth. The Word says in Proverbs 4:23 — "Guard your heart above all else, for everything you do flows from it." Your words are a gateway to your heart. What goes out of your mouth is connected to what lives inside you. So guard it. Protect it. Make the decision that your words belong to God.

Step 3 — Declaration

This is where the power is. Once you catch yourself about to agree with the negative — counter it with the Word. You do not need a long speech. You do not need to correct anyone. You simply need your own declaration ready. Find your Romans 8:28. Find the scripture that speaks directly to what the enemy keeps trying to get you to agree with — and make it your automatic response. Speak it in the mirror in the morning. Speak it in the car. Speak it quietly under your breath in that conversation when someone is waiting for you to co-sign their defeat.

Here are a few examples to get you started:

When someone says *"nothing ever works out"* — you declare:

> *"When I tell you — all things work together for my good, believe me. I have seen it too many times to doubt it now."*

When someone says *"everybody is struggling out here"* — you declare:

> *"Well, I will say this — I am so appreciative to God for how He has been providing for me. I cannot thank Him enough."*

When someone says *"you can't trust anybody these days"* — you declare:

> *"My trust is in God. And He covers me. He has never once left me exposed."*

When someone says *"if it ain't one thing it's another"* — you declare:

> *"I used to say that too. But not anymore. Because God keeps turning things around for me."*

You are not ignoring reality. You are choosing a higher reality. You are choosing the reality that God already established for you before the foundation of the world. That is not denial. That is faith. And faith always wins.

The Words Stop Here

Nobody handed you a manual when you were growing up that said "these words will limit your life." The people who spoke them over you did not know. Their parents did not know. And their parents before them did not know either. It was simply what was spoken, what was heard, what was believed and what was passed down.

But the cycle ends with you.

You now know that your words are not neutral. They are not just filler in a conversation or a polite way to relate to someone going through a hard time. Your words are seeds. And every seed produces after its own kind. You have been planting without realizing it. And you have been harvesting exactly what you planted.

The good news is that the same principle that worked against you will now work for you. Because now you are going to plant something different. You are going to open your mouth with intention. You are going to guard what you agree with. You are going to counter the negative with the truth of God's Word — not in a preachy way, not in a religious way, but in a real, lived, *I have seen it work* kind of way.

The words that were spoken over you do not get to define you. Only the Word of God gets that authority. And He says you are covered. Provided for. Protected. Favored. Healed. Whole.

Now start saying it like you believe it.

Chapter 2 — The Danger of Negative Agreement

Sometimes you do not realize how powerful agreement is until it costs you something.

I learned that lesson the hard way — in a car dealership parking lot, watching a car I thought was mine get driven away.

A close friend of mine had been through it just weeks before. She had been approved for a car, driven it off the lot, felt that excitement of something new — only to have the dealership call her two days later and take it back. Financing had fallen through. The joy turned into embarrassment and disappointment almost overnight.

Then it was my turn. I went through the process, got approved, drove off the lot. And that same friend looked at me and said, "Don't get too comfortable. You saw what they did to me. Let me ride in it and think it was mine, only to turn around and take it back."

And instead of countering it — instead of declaring what I believed God had for me — I agreed.

> *"Yes, these dealerships these days are shady.*
> *Always looking for a reason to renege on a deal."*

Two days later they took my car back. Same reason. Financing denied. And my friend was right there.

"I told you so."

I was devastated. Not just because of the car — but something in my spirit knew. I had opened my mouth and agreed with exactly what I did not want to see. And I saw it.

As I watched my car drive away, I spoke to God internally. "God, you see this, right?" I was not begging. I was not listing everything that went wrong. I acknowledged what was and I listened. Then from somewhere deep within, I turned to my friend and told her, "They are going to give me my car back."

She went silent. Not an encouraging silence. The kind of silence that says *I don't want to tell you that you're wrong, but I think you're wrong*. But I did not need her agreement this time. I had already agreed with God.

I walked into that dealership and asked for the manager. I explained my situation and asked for a resolution. When I finished, I could tell he was surprised by my words. But his reply was still the same — they were keeping the car. I walked out of that dealership with my head held high. Confident. Unbothered. And I turned to my friend and said — "They are going to call me first thing in the morning to tell me to come get my car."

The next morning, at 7:59am — one minute before they opened — my phone rang.

It was the manager.

> *"Come get your car."*

What Just Happened

Let me break down what took place in that moment — because there is a lesson layered in every part of it.

When my friend spoke those words of doubt over my situation, she was not trying to hurt me. She was speaking from her own pain, her own experience, her own disappointment. That is important to understand. Most people who pull you into negative agreement are not your enemies. They are wounded people speaking wounded words. They genuinely believe what they are saying because they lived it. But their experience does not have to become your declaration.

The moment I agreed with her — I opened a door.

And the enemy walked right through it.

This is the danger of agreement that most people never talk about. It does not always come from a stranger. It does not always come from someone with bad intentions. Sometimes it comes from the people closest to you. The ones who love you. The ones who are trying to protect you from the same hurt they felt. But love wrapped around a faithless word is still a faithless word. And when you agree with it — you give it power in your life.

Amos 3:3 asks — "Can two walk together unless they are agreed?" That scripture is usually applied to relationships. But it is also a spiritual principle. Agreement creates partnership. And whatever you partner with — you will walk with. You will live with. You will see manifest in your life.

I partnered with doubt. And doubt delivered exactly what it promised.

But the moment I stopped listing the problem and got quiet before God — everything changed. That something deep within that rose up in me was not random. It was God. And when I opened my mouth and declared out loud to my friend — "They are going to give me my car back" — I shifted my agreement from doubt to faith.

And here is what I want you to notice. I walked into that dealership, explained my situation and asked for a resolution. The manager was surprised by my words. But his answer was still no. I walked out with no car, no approval and no guarantee — except the declaration I had already made. And I held onto it. I went to sleep that night not on the basis of what I could see — but on the basis of what I had declared. Because I AM not moved by what I see. Only by what I believe.

That is faith. Not the feeling. Not the evidence. Not the manager's approval. Just the Word. Just the declaration. Just the agreement between me and God.

And at 7:59am — God showed up.

He will do the same for you. But you have to be willing to do what I did in that parking lot. Stop agreeing with what you see. Stop partnering with what hurts. Get quiet before God, listen for that something deep within, and then open your mouth and declare it — even when the answer is still no. Even when the silence from the people around you is deafening. Even when you walk away with nothing in your hands.

Declare it anyway. Because what is in your mouth is more powerful than what is in front of your eyes.

The Agreement You Make Today

Every single day you are presented with a choice. Someone will say something. Something will happen. A report will come back negative. A door will close. A friend will look at you with that silence that says *I don't think this is going to work out for you.* And in that moment you will have to decide — what are you going to agree with?

Because you are always agreeing with something. There is no neutral ground. Every word you speak, every statement you co-sign, every conversation you walk away from without countering — you have cast a vote. For or against yourself. For or against what God has promised you. For or against the life you are declaring or the life you are dreading.

The enemy understands this better than most believers do. He is not always going to come at you with something obvious. He is not always going to show up as a clear attack. Sometimes he shows up as a concerned friend. A familiar saying. A reasonable sounding doubt. And all he needs is your agreement. Just a "you're right, it is what it is." That is all it takes to open the door.

But you know better now. And knowing changes everything.

From this day forward, guard your agreements like they are the most valuable thing you own — because spiritually, they are. Be intentional about what you co-sign. Be selective about what you allow to settle in your spirit through your own mouth. And when doubt comes knocking — and it will come knocking — answer it with a declaration.

Not because everything looks perfect. Not because the manager said yes. Not because the situation changed overnight. But because you are not moved by what you see. Only by what you believe.

That is the agreement that changes everything.

Chapter 3 — Counter With Your Truth

There is a moment that comes in every battle. A moment where you have to decide — am I going to respond to this or am I going to react to it? Reacting is automatic. It is what you have always done. It is the nod, the agreement, the "you're right, it never works out." But responding — responding requires intention. It requires preparation. It requires knowing what you believe before the moment arrives.

That is what this chapter is about. Not just knowing that your words are powerful — you already know that now. But knowing exactly what to say when the pressure is on. When the report is bad. When the friend is waiting for you to agree. When the situation looks impossible. When everything in you wants to react the way you always have.

This is where your truth comes in.

What Is Your Truth?

Your truth is not what you see. Your truth is not what you feel. Your truth is not the doctor's report, the bank statement, the relationship status or the opinion of anyone who has ever doubted you. Your truth is what God has already said about you. It was established before you were born. It was settled before the problem ever showed up. And it is available to you right now — in the Word of God.

Romans 8:28 says — "And we know that all things work together for good to those who love God, to those who are called according to His purpose."

All things. Not some things. Not the easy things. Not the things that make sense. All things. That means the car that got taken back. The job that fell through. The relationship that ended. The diagnosis that came back wrong. All of it — every single bit of it — is working together for your good. That is not a feeling. That is not positive thinking. That is the Word of the living God. And when you speak it — you are not just encouraging yourself. You are activating a promise that was already made on your behalf.

That is your foundation. That is your first counter. When life comes at you and everything looks like it is falling apart — "All things work together for my good." Say it like you mean it. Say it like you have seen it work. Say it like you believe it even when you do not yet feel it.

Because here is the secret — you do not have to feel it to say it. You just have to say it until you feel it.

Finding Your Personal Counter Scripture

Romans 8:28 is a powerful starting place. But God's Word is full of promises that speak directly to every area of your life.

Part of building your declaration life is finding the scriptures that speak to what you are facing and making them personal. Making them yours.

Take the area where the enemy attacks you most. Where the negative agreement shows up most often. Where the old sayings have the most grip on your life. And find the scripture that directly contradicts it. Then rewrite it in the first person. Make it a declaration. Speak it out loud every single day until it becomes more real to you than the problem ever was.

Here are some examples to get you started:

When the attack is on your finances —

> *Philippians 4:19 — "My God shall supply all your need according to His riches in glory."*
>
> *"My God supplies every need I have. I do not lack. I do not struggle. I am provided for in every area of my life. My finances are blessed and increasing."*

When the attack is on your protection and reputation —

> *Isaiah 54:17 — "No weapon formed against you shall prosper, and every tongue which rises against you in judgment you shall condemn."*
>
> *"No weapon formed against me shall prosper. Every word spoken against me falls to the ground. My reputation is protected. My integrity speaks for itself. I AM honest. I AM trustworthy. I AM covered."*

When the attack is on your health —

Isaiah 53:5 — "By His stripes you are healed."

"I AM healed. My body functions at a level of excellence. Every organ, every system, every cell operates the way God designed it to. Every report going forward is a good report. I AM healthy and whole."

When the attack is on your purpose and direction —

Jeremiah 29:11 — "For I know the plans I have for you, declares the Lord, plans to prosper you and not to harm you, plans to give you hope and a future."

"God has a plan for my life and it is good. I am not lost. I am not behind. I am not too late. Every step I take is ordered by God. My future is secure and my purpose is unfolding perfectly."

When the attack is on your peace of mind —

Philippians 4:7 — "The peace of God, which surpasses all understanding, will guard your hearts and minds."

"I have the peace of God. My mind is clear. My heart is steady. I do not operate in fear or anxiety. I AM calm. I AM focused. I AM at peace."

Speaking It With Confidence When You Do Not Feel It

This is the part nobody talks about. What do you do when you open your mouth to declare and everything inside you feels like a liar? When the situation is so heavy that the words feel hollow? When you say "I AM healed" and your body is screaming otherwise?

You say it anyway.

Not because you are ignoring reality. Not because you are pretending everything is fine. But because you have made a decision about which reality gets the final word. The seen or the unseen. The temporary or the eternal. What the problem says or what God says.

Hebrews 11:1 tells us that "faith is the substance of things hoped for, the evidence of things not seen." Faith is not the feeling. Faith is the decision to speak what you believe before you see what you believe. Every single person in the Bible who received a miracle had to speak and act before they saw the result. The walls of Jericho did not fall before the people marched. The Red Sea did not part before Moses stretched out his rod. The car did not come back before I declared it would.

The declaration comes first. The manifestation follows.

So when you do not feel it — speak it louder. Not out of desperation. Out of conviction. Out of the settled knowledge that God's Word does not return void. Isaiah 55:11 promises — "My word that goes out from my mouth will not return to me empty, but will accomplish what I desire and achieve the purpose for which I sent it." That Word in your mouth is the same Word. Speak it with that kind of confidence.

Building Your Daily Declaration Habit

Declarations are not just for crisis moments. They are not something you pull out only when the car gets taken back or the doctor's report comes in wrong. They are a lifestyle. A daily practice. A way of training your mouth — and your mind — to default to the truth of God rather than the noise of the world.

Every morning before your feet hit the floor — speak. Before you check your phone, before you turn on the news, before the world gets a chance to set the tone for your day — open your mouth and declare who you are and what God has promised you.

Start with these and make them your own:

> *"This is the day the Lord has made. I will rejoice and be glad in it."*
>
> *"I AM blessed coming in and blessed going out."*
>
> *"I AM the head and not the tail. Above only and not beneath."*
>
> *"Everything I put my hand to today prospers."*
>
> *"I AM loved. I AM protected. I AM provided for. I AM healed. I AM whole."*
>
> *"All things — ALL things — are working together for my good."*

Speak it in the morning. Speak it in the car. Speak it when the negative thought comes. Speak it when someone tries to pull you into agreement with defeat. Speak it until it is the most natural thing in the world. Speak it until your default response to every attack is the Word of God.

Because here is what happens when you build that habit — you stop being surprised by the goodness of God. You start expecting it. And what you expect, you prepare for. And what you prepare for, you receive.

Chapter 4 — How to Pray With Authority

Most people were never taught how to pray. They were taught to bow their head, close their eyes and talk to God — and that is a beautiful place to start. But somewhere along the way prayer became a one sided conversation where we did all the talking and most of what we said was a list of everything wrong. A running report of every problem, every fear, every situation that needed fixing. And then we said amen and waited.

But prayer was never designed to be a complaint session. It was designed to be a conversation between a child and a Father who has already made provision for everything His child will ever need. Before you were born. Before the problem showed up. Before the diagnosis, the financial pressure, the broken relationship or the closed door — God had already made a promise that covered it.

Your job in prayer is not to inform God of the problem. He already knows. Your job is to let Him know that you remember His promise — and then declare it over your life with the confidence of someone who believes their Father keeps His word.

That is praying with authority.

The Difference Between Begging and Believing

There is a version of prayer that sounds humble but is actually rooted in doubt. It goes something like this –

> *"God I don't know what I'm going to do. Things are so hard right now. I've been trying and nothing is working. Please, please help me. I just need you to fix this. I don't know how much more I can take."*

Notice what that prayer is doing. It is declaring defeat. It is declaring confusion. It is declaring limitation. And by the end of it you feel worse than when you started because you have just spent five minutes rehearsing everything that is wrong.

Now here is that same situation prayed with authority –

> *"Father, Your Word says that You will never leave me nor forsake me. You said that You are my refuge and my strength, a very present help in times of trouble. I thank You that You see exactly where I am and You already have a way out. I declare that this situation is turning around for my good. I declare that the answer is available to me now. I AM not confused. I AM not defeated. I AM not alone. You are with me and that is enough."*

Same situation. Same person. Completely different prayer. The first one ends in desperation. The second one ends in faith. The first one reminds you of the problem. The second one reminds God — and yourself — of the promise.

That is the shift. That is what this chapter is about.

How To Remind God of His Word

Reminding God of His Word is not about informing Him of something He forgot. God does not forget. It is about you coming into alignment with what He has already said. It is about building your faith as you pray by speaking His promises out loud. It is about establishing in the atmosphere — in your home, in your body, in your mind — that you believe what God said more than you believe what you see.

Here is the framework. Three simple steps that will transform the way you pray:

Step 1 — Acknowledge God First

Before you bring anything else — bring Him. Not the problem. Not the list. Him. Thank Him for who He is. Establish in your spirit that you are coming before a God who is able, willing and already working on your behalf.

> *"Father, I come before You today grateful. You are God and there is none like You. You are able to do exceedingly and abundantly above all that I could ask or think. I trust You completely."*

Step 2 — Remind Him of His Promise

Find the scripture that speaks directly to your situation and bring it before God. Not as a demand — but as a child who knows their Father's word and stands on it with confidence.

> *"Father, Your Word says in Jeremiah 29:11 that You have plans for me. Plans to prosper me and not to harm me. Plans to give me hope and a future. I stand on that promise today."*

> *"Father, Your Word says that by the stripes of Jesus I AM healed. That is not my opinion — that is Your Word. And I stand on it."*

Step 3 — Declare It Over Your Life

This is where prayer becomes declaration. After you have acknowledged God and reminded Him of His promise — speak it over yourself. Out loud. With conviction. With the authority of someone who knows they are a child of the Most High God.

> *"So I declare today that my future is secure. I declare that my health is restored. I declare that my finances are blessed and increasing. I declare that every door that needs to open is opening and every door that needs to close is closing. I declare that I AM walking in purpose, in peace and in power. Because You said it — and Your Word does not return void."*

What Happens When You Pray This Way

Something shifts when you pray with authority. Not just in your circumstances — but in you. When you spend time reminding God of His promises, you end up reminding yourself. Your faith grows. Your confidence rises. Your perspective changes. The problem does not disappear the moment you say amen — but you are no longer the same person who started the prayer. You walked in overwhelmed and you walk out anchored.

That is what prayer is supposed to do. Not just move God — but move you. From fear to faith. From doubt to declaration. From begging to believing.

Hebrews 4:16 tells us to "come boldly to the throne of grace, that we may obtain mercy and find grace to help in time of need." Boldly. Not timidly. Not apologetically. Not with a list of reasons why you might not deserve the answer. Boldly. With the confidence of a child who knows their Father loves them and has already made provision for everything they need.

That is your posture in prayer. Bold. Grateful. Expectant. Declaring what you believe before you see what you believe.

Because the prayer of a righteous person is powerful and effective. And you are righteous — not because of anything you did — but because of everything He did. So pray like it.

The Prayer That Changes Everything

There is a version of you that has not yet shown up. A version that walks into every situation anchored. That responds to every attack with a declaration. That opens their mouth every morning and sets the tone for the day before the world gets a chance to. A version that prays not from a place of desperation but from a place of authority. Not begging. Believing.

That version of you is not far away. It is one decision away. The decision to never again walk into prayer with just a list of problems — but to walk in with the Word of God in your mouth and the promises of your Father in your heart.

You do not have to have it all figured out. You do not have to feel strong. You do not have to have the perfect words. You just have to show up before God, remind Him of what He promised, and declare it over your life like you believe it.

Because here is what I have learned. God is not looking for perfect prayers. He is looking for faithful ones. Prayers that say — "Father I do not see how this works out, but Your Word says it will. And I choose Your Word over what I see." That kind of prayer moves heaven. That kind of prayer silences the enemy. That kind of prayer changes you from the inside out.

So from this day forward — pray with authority. Acknowledge your Father. Remind Him of His Word. And declare what you want to see over your life every single day until what you see catches up with what you believe.

Because it will.

Chapter 5 — Speaking What You Want to See: Faith Declarations in Action

By the time you reach this chapter, you have done the work. You have identified the words you inherited. You have recognized the danger of agreement. You have learned to counter with your truth and pray with authority. Now it is time to put it all together and watch it move.

This chapter is about faith declarations in action. Not just what you say in a crisis. Not just what you pray when the car gets taken back or the doctor's report comes in wrong. But what you speak over your life every single day — in the ordinary, in the routine, in the middle of a commute you hate and a job that is draining the life out of you.

Because that is exactly where this works.

The Declaration That Changed My Days

I had a job I hated.

Not the kind of dislike that fades after a good weekend. The deep, exhausting, soul-draining kind. Every morning I faced an hour in traffic just to get there. Every evening I fought rush hour traffic for an hour and a half to get back home. And in between — unpleasant people, difficult environments and a daily grind that felt like it was squeezing something out of me that I could not get back.

But instead of declaring my misery — I started declaring my freedom.

Every morning, before I walked into that day, I spoke over my life. Out loud. With intention. With vision:

> *"I am free to do whatever I want during the day. I do not have to get out in traffic to get to work. I can schedule my day as I please. Freedom is mine. God said I can name my day, so I call this day full of freedom to do as I please."*

And then I did something powerful. I sat with it. I closed my eyes and I envisioned what that freedom looked like. What it felt like to wake up and own my time. To move through my day without the weight of traffic and tension and difficult people. I let myself feel it before I had seen it. And it started my day right — every single day.

Then I went to work. As usual. No dramatic exit. No quitting in faith. Just a woman with a word in her mouth and a vision in her heart, doing what needed to be done while believing that what she declared was already in motion.

And then God moved.

COVID changed everything. My job changed from in office to work from home. Overnight the commute disappeared. The unpleasant people no longer had access to me. The traffic that had been stealing hours from my life every day — gone. That was the first layer of the blessing.

Then my husband secured a lucrative contract. And I was able to leave that job altogether.

Now my days are full of freedom. I wake up and I schedule my day as I please. I am not fighting traffic. I am not surrounded by people who drain me. I am living the exact life I declared over myself — word for word, vision for vision.

That is not coincidence. That is not luck. That is the Word working.

What Made It Work

There are a few things I want you to notice about that declaration that made it powerful. Because it was not random. It was intentional. And the same principles that worked for me will work for you.

First — I declared it in the present tense. Not "one day I will be free." Not "I hope things get better." I said "I AM free. Freedom is mine. I call this day full of freedom." Present tense. As if it already existed. Because in the spirit — it already did. God had already made provision for it. My declaration was simply bringing it from the invisible into the visible.

Second — I gave it a vision. After I spoke it I sat with it. I let myself see it. Feel it. Experience it before I had evidence of it. This is not daydreaming. This is faith with a picture. Habakkuk 2:2 says "Write the vision and make it plain." God instructed His people to see it clearly enough to write it down. When you can see your declaration in your mind — when you can feel what it feels like to live it — you are not just speaking words. You are building a reality.

Third — I kept showing up. I did not quit my job the day after I made that declaration. I kept doing what was in front of me to do — faithfully, consistently — while holding my declaration in my heart. That is what faith looks like in real life. It is bold belief paired with faithful action.

And fourth — I let God determine the method. I did not tell God how to bring my freedom. I simply declared the outcome and trusted God with the path. And He used something none of us saw coming — a global pandemic — to begin the process of setting me free. God's methods will always surprise you. Your job is to declare the destination and trust Him with the route.

Speaking Over Every Area of Your Life

Your declaration life is not limited to one area. God's promises cover every part of who you are — your health, your relationships, your finances, your purpose, your peace and your family. And every single one of those areas deserves to hear your voice speaking life over it.

Family and Relationships

> *"My family is covered by the blood of Jesus. My home is a place of peace, love and safety. My relationships are healthy, whole and rooted in God. I attract people of integrity, loyalty and love into my life. Every broken relationship in my family is being healed. My children walk in purpose and are protected in every direction they go. My marriage is strong, blessed and growing. We are for each other and God is for us."*

Health and Healing

> *"I AM healed from the crown of my head to the soles of my feet. My body is the temple of the Holy Spirit and it functions at a level of excellence. Every organ, every system, every cell operates exactly the way God designed it to. I do not receive a bad report. I declare that every doctor's visit going forward confirms what I already know — I AM healthy, whole and well. By His stripes I AM healed and I walk in that healing every single day."*

Finances and Provision

"My God supplies all of my needs according to His riches in glory. I do not lack. I do not struggle. Money flows to me consistently and abundantly. Every bill is paid. Every need is met. I AM a good steward of what God has entrusted to me and He keeps entrusting me with more. Doors of financial opportunity are opening for me right now. I AM blessed and a blessing to others."

Purpose and Destiny

"I know why I AM here. My purpose is clear and I AM walking in it boldly. Every gift God placed in me is being activated and used for His glory. I AM not too late. I have not missed my moment. God's plan for my life is unfolding perfectly and on His timeline. Every step I take is ordered by God. I AM exactly where I need to be and I AM becoming everything He created me to be."

Peace of Mind

"I have the mind of Christ. I do not operate in fear, anxiety or confusion. My mind is clear. My thoughts are steady. I cast down every thought that does not align with the Word of God. I AM at peace. I AM focused. I AM emotionally whole and spiritually strong. No weapon of the mind formed

against me shall prosper. I think clearly, speak clearly and live clearly."

Daily Freedom and Quality of Life

"My days are full of purpose and freedom. I wake up with energy and intention. I move through my day with grace and ease. The right people, the right opportunities and the right resources show up at the right time. Everything I put my hand to prospers. God orders my steps and directs my path. This is a good day. I declare it good before it even begins."

This Is How You Live Now

You have come a long way from that conversation at the beginning of this book. The one where someone laid out everything going wrong and waited for you to nod and agree. You are not that person anymore. You are someone who knows the power of their words. Someone who guards their agreements. Someone who opens their mouth with intention and declares what they want to see before they see it.

And now you have seen it work.

I was a woman who hated her commute but did not quit my job in the many moments of frustration. I declared my freedom every single morning and then went to work. I spoke it. I envisioned it. I trusted God with the method. And one day

I woke up and realized I was living the exact life I had been declaring — word for word, vision for vision.

That is available to you. Not someday. Now. Starting today. Starting with the very next words that come out of your mouth.

This is not a seasonal practice. This is a lifestyle. A complete rewiring of the way you think, the way you speak and the way you move through the world. It requires consistency. It requires conviction. And on the days when everything in you wants to react instead of declare — it requires a decision.

Choose your words. Every single day. Over your health, your family, your finances, your purpose and your peace. Speak them in the morning before the world has a chance to set the tone. Speak them in the car when the old thoughts try to creep back in. Speak them in the middle of the hard conversation when someone is waiting for you to co-sign their defeat.

You were not built to co-sign darkness. You were built to declare light.

So open your mouth. Speak what you want to see. And then watch God move.

Because He will.

Conclusion — Now Open Your Mouth

You picked up this book because something in you knew there had to be a better way.

Maybe you were exhausted from praying the same prayers and seeing the same results. Maybe you were tired of agreeing with everything going wrong around you and feeling the weight of it in your own life. Maybe you just had a feeling — a quiet, persistent knowing — that your words were more powerful than you had been treating them.

You were right.

What you have learned in these pages is not a new concept. It is an ancient principle woven through the Word of God from beginning to end. In the beginning God spoke — and what He spoke came into existence. He did not survey the darkness and agree with it. He did not list everything that was void and formless and wait for someone to fix it. He opened His mouth and declared what He wanted to see.

And it was so.

You are made in His image. And that means you carry that same creative power in your mouth. Every word you speak is either building something or tearing something down. Every agreement you make is either opening a door or closing one.

Every declaration you release into the atmosphere is either moving you toward the life God promised you or away from it.

Now you know. And knowing is not enough — doing is everything.

So here is your charge as you close this book and step back into your life:

Watch what you agree with. The moment someone tries to pull you into a conversation that ends in defeat — counter it. Not with argument. Not with a sermon. Just with your truth. A quiet, confident, I-have-seen-it-work declaration that reminds the atmosphere who you are and what God has already said about you.

Remind God of His Word. Walk into your prayer time not with a list of problems but with a heart full of His promises. Acknowledge Him. Remind Him of what He said. And then declare it over your life with the boldness of a child who trusts their Father completely.

Speak what you want to see. Every single day. Over every area of your life. Your health. Your family. Your finances. Your purpose. Your peace. Your freedom. Speak it in the morning. Speak it at noon. Speak it when the enemy tries to remind you of what it used to look like. Speak it until you are living it.

Because the life God has for you is not a mystery. It is a declaration away.

You have the Word. You have the authority. You have the promise.

Now open your mouth.

ONLY SPEAK WHAT YOU WANT TO SEE.

Bonus Declaration Prayers

These declarations are yours. Speak them out loud. Speak them with conviction. Speak them every day until they are more familiar to you than the negative words you used to agree with. Make them personal. Make them yours. And watch what happens.

Morning Declarations — Set the Tone Before the World Does

"This is the day the Lord has made. I will rejoice and be glad in it."

"I AM blessed coming in and blessed going out."

"Everything I put my hand to today prospers."

"I AM the head and not the tail. Above only and not beneath."

"Favor surrounds me like a shield today."

"The right people, the right opportunities and the right resources are coming my way today."

"God orders my steps and I will not miss a single one."

"This is a good day. I declare it good before it even begins."

Declarations Against Fear

"I did not receive a spirit of fear. I operate in power, love and a sound mind."

"I AM confident that God is my protector."

"I AM safe."

"What God has for me cannot be stopped by what I am facing right now."

"I AM covered. I AM protected. I AM at peace."

Declarations Against Lack

"My God supplies ALL of my needs. Every single one."

"I do not lack. I do not struggle. I AM provided for completely."

"Money flows to me consistently and abundantly."

"Every bill is paid. Every need is met. Every door of opportunity is open."

"I AM blessed and a blessing to others."

"Lack is not my portion. Abundance is my inheritance."

Declarations Against Sickness

"By the stripes of Jesus I AM healed."

"My body is the temple of the Holy Spirit and it functions perfectly."

"Every organ, every system, every cell operates the way God designed it to."

"I do not receive a bad report. I only receive good news."

"Sickness has no place in this body. Health and healing are mine."

"I AM whole. I AM strong. I AM well."

Declarations Against Doubt

"I believe the Word of God more than I believe what I see."

"I AM not moved by circumstances. I AM moved by faith."

"God has never failed me and He will not start now."

"I have seen it work too many times to doubt it now."

"All things — ALL things — are working together for my good."

Declarations for Family and Relationships

"My home is a place of peace, love and safety."

"My family is covered and protected in every direction."

"My children walk in purpose and are guarded by the hand of God."

"My marriage is strong, blessed and growing every day."

"I attract people of integrity, loyalty and love into my life."

"Every broken relationship in my family is being healed."

"My house and everyone in it — we serve the Lord."

Declarations for Purpose and Destiny

"I know why I am here and I AM walking in it boldly."

"I am not too late. I have not missed my moment."

"Every gift God placed in me is activated and being used."

"My purpose is unfolding perfectly on God's timeline."

"I AM exactly where I need to be."

"Greater things are coming. The best is still ahead."

"I AM becoming everything God created me to be."

A Daily Declaration to Carry With You

"I AM covered. I AM healed. I AM provided for. I AM protected. I AM loved. I AM purposed. I AM free. God is for me, and if God is for me — nothing

and no one can stand against me. This is my day. And I only speak what I want to see."

About the Author

MRS. JAE is a woman of faith, vision and purpose whose words have a way of stopping a room.

It was at a millionaire roundtable — a gathering of high achievers pursuing their best lives — that this book was born. On the final day, participants were asked to share in one sentence the message they most wanted to give to the world. Without hesitation, she said: *"**Only Speak What You Want To See**."*

The room erupted. Someone shouted, *"That's the name of your book!"* She laughed and said no. And the entire room said, *"It should be."*

She knew they were right. And in less than a month, she wrote it.

Drawing from personal testimony, lived faith and the unshakeable promises of God's Word, MRS. JAE writes with the conviction of someone who has not just studied these principles — but lived them. From declaring a repossessed car back into her driveway to speaking her way out of a job she hated into a life of freedom, every word in this book is backed by real experience.

She is also at work on her memoir, *A Flower Amongst Trees* — a deeply personal story that has been years in the making and promises to be just as transformative.

Only Speak What You Want To See is her first published book. It will not be her last.

Made in the USA
Coppell, TX
30 June 2026

83852145R00027